Jesus and the cheat

by Diane Walker

"Look! There's Zacchaeus!" Mark shouted.

They had spotted Zacchaeus, handing over the tax money he had collected.

"And there's Zacchaeus' brave guard, looking after him!" Rachel said. "Daren't you go out alone?" she mocked the man in the rich clothes.

"That's not his guard – that's his friend!" Mark laughed. "In fact, it's his only friend!"

"You're right!" Rachel agreed. "Only a Roman would be friends with him – and *he* has to be paid to do it, too! None of *us* would be friends with a man like Zacchaeus. Come on! Mum's waiting for that new dish. Trust you to break the old one!"

They ran off, Mark explaining that it wasn't his fault he had dropped the dish. The goat had knocked him over.

Zacchaeus had heard everything. He watched the children run off to the market, pushing and tugging at each other like puppies. He remembered how, when he was young, he had happily run errands for other people. Now no one would ask a favour of him. In fact, people only spoke to him when they had to, and then it was usually to beg him for more time to pay their taxes.

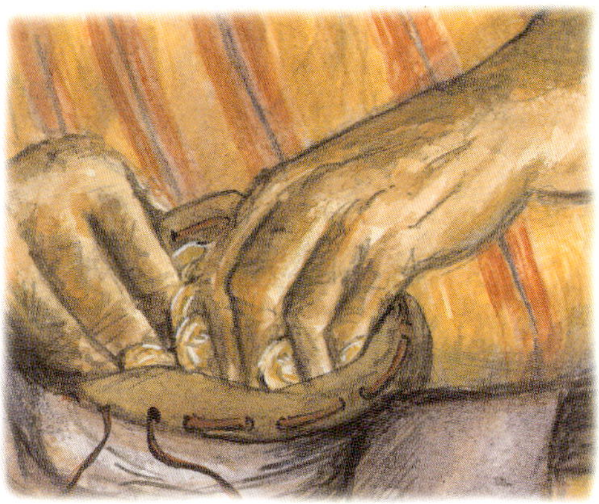

He set off down the street, glancing sideways to see if the soldier was watching him. But the soldier was watching an elderly woman struggling to carry a full water jar. Quickly, Zacchaeus hid the coins he had taken for himself in his own secret money bag, that he kept hidden. He smiled to himself.

"I don't care what people think," he thought. "I don't need them. I'm not like them, working like ants to make enough money to buy cheap pots from the market. Nothing but the best for me! I know how to look after myself."

"We'll go to Simon the potter next," he told the soldier. "He still owes some of last month's money as well as this. He'll be at his market stall outside his workshop. Come on."

Simon waved goodbye to Rachel and her brother. They had carefully chosen just the dish they needed to replace the one Mark had broken. They had counted out the small coins into Simon's clay-covered hands and then cheerfully run off.

"Don't break that one, too!" he had shouted after them, and Mark, grinning, had turned and waved.

"We won't!" he yelled, and hurried to catch up with his sister.

Simon smiled, and went back to his workbench. He dropped the few coins into his money bag. It felt very light. A shadow fell across the stall. He looked up: it was Zacchaeus.

"I hope you've sold more than that dish!" Zacchaeus said, frowning at the pottery in distaste. "Let's see how much you've got!"

Simon replied sadly, "This is all I have. Is it enough?"

He emptied the coins into the tax collector's outstretched hands.

Zacchaeus quickly calculated how much there was. It was enough: in fact, it was exactly the amount the Romans had demanded from the potter. But that would mean Zacchaeus himself would get nothing. He looked up at Simon's hopeful face.

"No," he said harshly, ignoring the disappointment on Simon's face, "it's not enough. I need another five silver coins." (For Zacchaeus had become rich by always taking more tax than he should, and squirrelling away the extra for himself.) "I'll give you just one more day, Simon, and then I'll have to take your poor little pottery to raise the money. Goodbye! Sleep well!"

He stalked off, the soldier trailing after him.

Simon watched him go. He picked up one of the pots. He felt the smoothness of the finished clay, and looked at the zigzag pattern round its edge. His father had always made that pattern, and had showed Simon how to do it too, years ago. It was like a sign, saying the pot was one of theirs. Now it was all coming to an end – all the years his family had worked here in this workshop.

"Simon. Simon!" He looked up. His friend Benjamin stood in front of him. "You were miles away," he said. "Listen! Jesus is here – in the main street. Are you coming?"

Jesus – here! Simon was excited and hurried off with his friend. They had all heard such stories about Jesus – how he taught so well that people listening to him even missed meals! People even said that Jesus had healed people. It would be wonderful to see him for themselves.

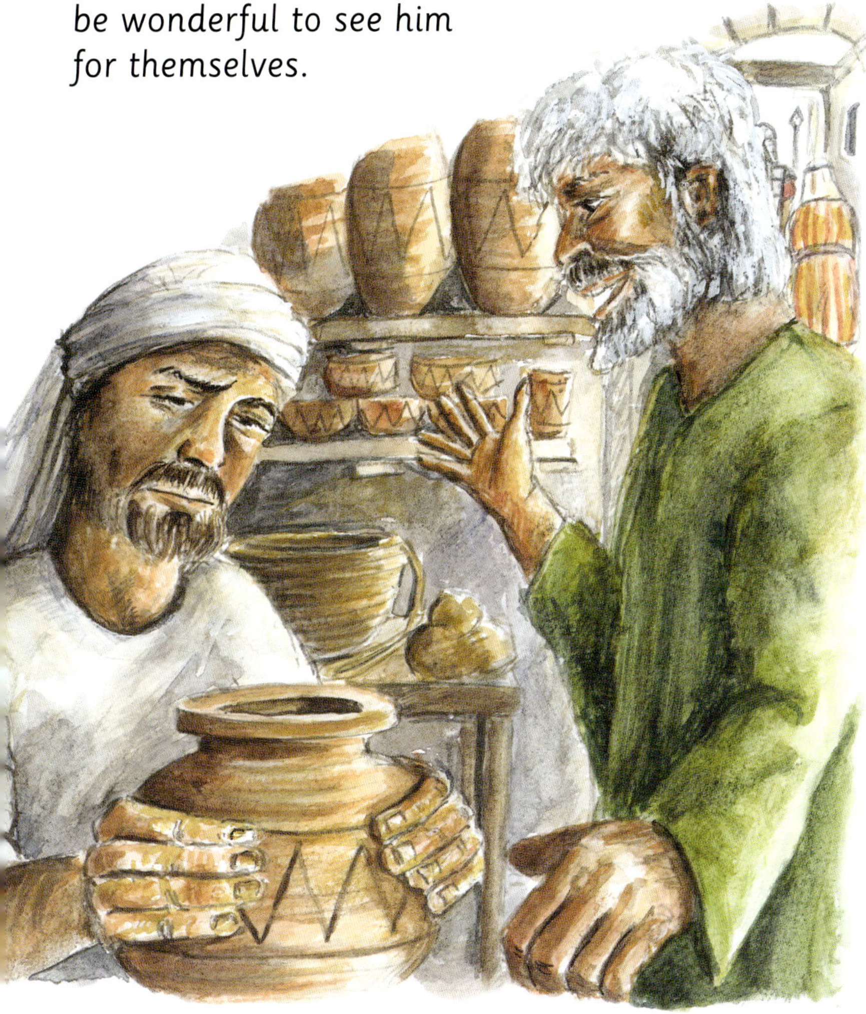

Meanwhile, Zacchaeus had seen the people hurrying to the main street. He caught a small boy by the ear as he rushed past, and made him tell him what was happening. Zacchaeus, too, had heard the stories about Jesus. He decided he must see this man. He sent the soldier off for his lunch, and hurried after the crowds. His money bag rattled quietly. There were many people there before him.

"Let me through!" he shouted.

At first, one or two people tried to move out of his way, but when they saw who it was, they closed up again, their backs like a wall in front of Zacchaeus.

Zacchaeus didn't know what to do. He was too short to see over their heads. He looked round desperately – and saw the old tree, its branches spread out like a tent over the street, bringing shade and a splash of green to the dusty road. Now he knew what to do. He tucked his robe into his belt. People might laugh at him, but he didn't care. Clumsily, he climbed the tree. He edged his way along one of the thick branches, over the street. Now Zacchaeus could see perfectly.

And here was Jesus, walking with a group of his friends down the street! Zacchaeus watched them carefully. Who was the man in the front? It looked like Bartimaeus, the blind man who begged every day at the town gate. But it couldn't be him! This man was rushing from one side of the street to the other like an excited child, shouting to anyone who would listen, "Look at me! I can see! He's healed me. Jesus has healed me!"

Zacchaeus couldn't believe it. Only yesterday he had had to reprimand the Roman soldier for throwing the blind man a coin. "Don't encourage him!" he had ordered. "And don't waste your money on rubbish like him!"

Now Bartimaeus could see!

Jesus was right underneath the tree now. Suddenly, he stopped. He looked up, beckoned, and said, "Zacchaeus! Hurry down. I want to come to your house!"

Zacchaeus couldn't believe it. For a moment, he couldn't move! Then, he squirmed down the tree, and hastily straightened his clothes.

"I would be honoured, Master!" he said, and led the way to his house, on the other, richer side of the town, well away from the noise and bustle of the main street.

Simon and Benjamin watched them go. They couldn't believe it either. "Did you see that?" Simon said.

"Well! Jesus can't have heard about him. He can't know what he's like – that he works for the Romans and cheats his own people!"

All around them, men and women were amazed that Jesus wanted to spend time with the selfish tax collector.

Zacchaeus was amazed, too. He clapped his hands for his servants to come, and ordered fresh water to wash Jesus' feet, cool drinks and rich food for his meal. He showed Jesus into the dining room, with its elegant couches, and invited him to use the softest, handing him a drink once he was settled. Zacchaeus couldn't believe this was happening!

Then Jesus started to talk. As he listened, Zacchaeus realised that Jesus knew all about him – even how he cheated others. But he also learned that Jesus still cared for him, despite everything.

Zacchaeus had thought he was used to having no friends. He had thought it was best to look after just himself. But now, he saw that life could be different – and that he could be different, too. And he learned that Jesus could help him to be different.

Suddenly, making money and looking after himself didn't seem so important. Now he wanted to please Jesus and to thank him for caring for him – and he knew how to do it!

He stood up. "Jesus, I'm sorry for the way I've lived. I see now that I have been wrong. I want to show other people how sorry I am. I want to help them instead of making them miserable. This is what I'm going to do. All the money which I've taken for myself from people, I'll repay four times over! What's more, I'll give to the poor half of everything I own."

It was quiet at Simon's house that evening. In silence, the unhappy family sat around the big pot of stew, dipping in it the warm crusty bread. Simon had explained to them that they would lose the pottery the next day.

Someone outside shouted Simon's name.

"That's Zacchaeus now!" Simon said, angrily. "Couldn't he even leave us alone tonight?"

He went out, and his family could hear the two men talking. They heard Zacchaeus shout his farewell.

Simon returned – and in his hand was a money bag.

"Hold out your hands, son," he whispered.

He untied the bag, tipped it upside down, and coins fell out, silver and gold, showering over his son's outstretched hands like metal rain. His wife watched as they cascaded to the earth floor, where they lay glinting in the light from the lamp.

"He gave them to me!" Simon said. "Zacchaeus gave them to me – coins to replace the ones he stole from me, and then even more coins to show how sorry he was for cheating us."

"Why?" asked his son. "Why is he giving away so much money?"

Simon shook his head.

His wife said, "It must have been Jesus! It seems that Bartimaeus isn't the only person whose life was changed by Jesus today."

"Yes," Simon said to his wife, "I think you're right."

He thought about the pottery and the new batch of dishes he could make the next day. It was time, he thought, to show his son how to make that zigzag pattern for himself.